On Guard

ministering Christ
in a messed-up world

Copyright 2015
Michael M. Middleton

Cover photo courtesy of Fontplay.com, used by permission.

Special thanks to Anthony Arriola, Aquatics Director,
South Sound YMCA, Briggs Community Branch

Special thanks also extended
to my "treading water" minions
on pages 75 and 99,
Aunya Gabo and Keenan Cain

Ben and Denise Charles,
founders of **Crazy Faith Outreach**,
one of a number of ministries
YWAM Faith Harvest Helpers
is blessed to partner with.

www.iamcrazyfaith.com

A Reason to Weep

The singer sang a sullen song –
mournful, deep, loud, and long.
The dancer danced a dreadful dirge,
maddened by the gruesome gong...
A mournful remembrance of priceless
mercy that they *would not* receive, a
pitiful protest against perfect truth that
they *would not* believe, forever will echo
in empty places from those who were
deceived. A fiery frost, when all is lost,
a grief *without* reprieve... All was offered,
all refused; all *would not believe.*

And in a time after time's end, He
ascends above all things to that place
where He, alone, dwells. He bears a
lonely sorrow, shielded from all other
hearts... a gnawing grief of shattered
hopes held for those who **would not** be
reached. The fullness of all glory...
secretly weeps.

Introduction:

Perhaps you would never guess it by some length of careful observation of my current physical appearance, but I have actually been a licensed lifeguard in two different states. Yes, my physique was once that of a supreme manhood and refined ruggedness... I possessed the debonair, just ever so slightly wind-blown hairdo of David Hasselhoff, as well as the suave sophistication of Errol Flynn. You begin to get closer to the full picture of my former glory when you add to this the back-woods ruggedness of Marvel Comic's *Wolverine* and a healthy dose of the mountain of muscular masculinity which is only hinted at in Arnold Schwarzenegger. And... and... and..........

Ok... not really. My physical appearance and general condition of manliness has, indeed, functioned on a higher plane in days —in decades‾ gone by, but even at my best, it was never really all that great. Though I always excelled academically, in the 'hunk' department, I was probably a solid C‾.

I do think that I was a pretty cute kid up to about the age of five or six. I even had kind of a James Dean look going early on... but it seems as though Sir Isaac Newton had it in for me and the universal law of entropy has made me its personal project. As with any middle‾aged man, I find myself caught in a slow, brutal, downhill slide into a deteriorating masculine mediocrity. All vain imaginations aside, my current fleshly abode is slipping away daily towards the land of short, fat, balding, and a tad too flatulent for polite company.

However, the part about having been a licensed lifeguard is true. In fact, I have been both a head lifeguard and a volunteer fireman. It is around the combination of these two experiences and my roughly twenty-five years of full-time ministry in various positions that this little book is framed. A lifeguard... a fireman... **any** first responder worth their salt will keep *this fact* always securely locked in the forefront of their minds on daily basis:

If you're dead, you can't help anyone!

Policemen, firemen, lifeguards, emergency medical technicians... all first responders are trained to protect their personal safety in all situations. Courage and devotion must be guided by reality, experience, and wisdom. You cannot help anyone if you are careless or hasty and become a victim yourself. In fact, instead of helping, you may very well become a burden and a danger to others.

These same principles apply to anyone involved in Christian ministry, be it from a professional, vocational standpoint or simply in the realm of personal evangelism. This is particularly true of those individuals reaching out to those farthest away from Christ and in most desperate need. Our hearts ache for such lost and damaged souls, but please remember... you cannot help anyone if you become a victim yourself. The world out there is already a pretty deadly minefield all on its own, and anyone seeking to extend the hope of Christ to those bound in the chains of hopelessness will soon attract the attention of a very clever and vicious adversary. Wisdom must guide compassion.

"Who Cares?"

In our modern world, this expression is often used as a statement rather than an honest question. It is frequently uttered in a derogatory tone... a flippant, belittling dismissal, meant to divert attention away from a valid argument against which the responder has no valid defense. However, one great father of the faith once spoke this short phrase in a much different voice.

William Booth, founder of The Salvation Army, once penned a message entitled, "Who Cares?". This bold and quite honestly heart-breaking exhortation has stood as a beacon down through the ages, calling into the field of Christian ministry men and women from across our little blue-green ball called "Earth". Rather than a dismissive utterance which seeks to escape a painful truth, it is a poignant and plaintive query which seeks to meet that truth head-on. The observations Mr. Booth made in this message are perhaps even more true today than when his pen first met paper. I will briefly summarize it here.

He writes a heart-stirring account of a vision given to him by God; a vision which dealt with God's broken heart over a lost and dying world... and His equal if not greater grief over a complacent church, which ignored His call to reach those lost and dying around them. In Booth's account, he saw a dark and violent sea, filled with desperate, dying people, lost in a mighty storm. They were crying out for help through the angry waves. In the midst of the sea, multitudes who had found safety on land... only recently rescued from destruction and death themselves... in large part ignored the desperate cries of those still lost in the angry sea. They were too caught up in worldly distractions and pleasures... and even in religious pursuits... to care for those still in desperation and danger. And so, soul after soul sank forever beneath the dark waves, as those safe on the shore busied themselves with pointless amusements and philosophical discussions. Only a few, a very precious few, were making an effort to respond to the cries of the dying.

> "The harvest truly is plentiful, but the laborers are few. Therefore, pray the Lord of the harvest to send more laborers into His harvest."
>
> Matthew 9:37-38

Yes, the Lord of the harvest desires that we be bold and courageous and that we partner with Him in rescuing the lost. But the burden of a lost and dying world is a heavy one --- one which we cannot bear ourselves. Nor are we supposed to; a frame which is merely human cannot carry such a load. Any attempt to do so will eventually break us. Like a lifeguard, our courage, compassion, and devotion must be matched and guided by training, teamwork, and wisdom. If we allow our heart to outpace our head, we will sooner or later find ourselves to be another victim in need of rescue.

In reaching out to a lost and dying world, we must not allow ourselves to become lost in their *lost-ness*. I have a sixteen year old son with the heart of Billy Graham. He is all about reaching out to his friends with the love and truth of Christ and does not shy away from those in very lost places in their lives. Sometimes, the weight of their situations and choices begins to weigh him down... and I see his heart begin to sink. I have begun to see that when he is angry or frustrated, it is just as often about this as it is about any 'typical' concerns of someone his age. His particular teenage-angst is frequently rooted in a tender heart for his friends and anger over those things weighing them down. Unfortunately, the weight of these concerns sometimes weighs too heavily on him, and he seems just barely able to keep his own head above water.

In praying about how to communicate the importance of guarding against this, the Lord brought back to my mind my days as a lifeguard and the various tactics and principles of keeping yourself safe as you attempt to help others in need. *You must always be aware of the whole picture... to rapidly assess your ability to respond to a perceived need and bear in mind the dangers of doing so... Know when someone actually needs physical help and when they just need some encouragement or direction... You must know, practice, and be able to quickly and effectively utilize such safety techniques as 'releases', 'escapes', and even 'plunges'...* methods of regaining control when a panicking victim begins to drag you under with them. Again, you cannot help anyone if you become a victim yourself.

Within these few pages I hope to serve a dual purpose: Firstly, to illustrate and further illuminate God's heart for a lost and dying world... and our rightful place as courageous co-laborers in reaching out to those yet lost in that dark and angry sea. Secondly, to communicate some few wise principles to help you keep your heart under the control of wisdom, so that you do not become another victim lost in the storm of life. This is not meant to be an exhaustive, scholarly, all-encompassing, seminary-level thesis. I simply hope to provide a few illustrations and exhortations to help you guard against allowing the weight of a lost world from dragging you beneath the waves of despair, resentment, or self-righteous bitterness as you go about the task of reaching a lost world for Christ. These principles and illustrations shall be presented in a brief, conversational or narrative form... as a father would speak to his son... as this is the heart which sparked this particular endeavor.

The best, truest, and most impactful presentation of truth is that which reaches beyond mere head knowledge and writes itself upon our hearts. In producing a discourse on Christian ministry I have, of course, employed relevant Scripture references throughout. I have also included, as established in the pages preceding this introduction, numerous works of poetry and prose appearing in my earlier books. Each of these is a brief glimpse of some facet or another of God's heart as he revealed it to me in times of prayer and quietness... whether in times of focused intercession, or simply taking a walk in the woods with "Daddy God..." I pray that they serve for you the purpose of fleshing out a fuller picture of God's heart for the lost and may perhaps illumine some aspect of how He may be calling you to participate in reaching those still desperately adrift in a dark and angry sea.

"Keep your heart with all diligence, for out of it spring the issues of life…"
Proverbs 4:23

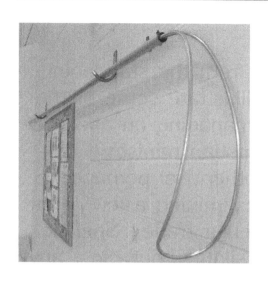

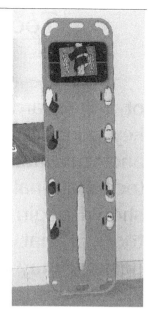

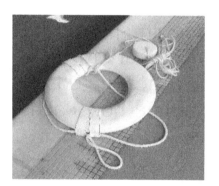

Tools of the Trade

If we are then, from the standpoint of a lifeguard, to illustrate some of the key principles of managing an affective and survivable Christian ministry (occupational or otherwise) perhaps we should begin by examining a few of the tools of that particular trade. Specific designs may vary slightly, but most any location with a certified lifeguard on duty will incorporate certain specific pieces of equipment necessary to the job. Let us indulge in a healthy dose of metaphor as we examine how each of these might apply to *our* particular endeavors of ministry.

The Whistle

The whistle---that bane of every mischievous pre-teen boy ever to patronize a city pool... This is perhaps the piece of equipment which lifeguards are best known for, the very representative definition and seal of lifeguard-dom. (Yes, I just made up that word, and I'm keeping it!) In its basic application the whistle means one thing: **STOP!**

One or two short blasts are usually implemented to get the attention of someone committing a minor infraction like running, dunking, swimming too close to the diving boards, or indulging in overactive horseplay. A shrill, sustained blast generally means one of two things. It may be an indication that someone is *really* busted and should probably claim their towel and call for a ride home. It could also be an indication of someone in serious need of rescue... essentially saying to all others in the water, **"Get outa' the way, I'm comin' in!"**

It can also be an indication, on rare occasions, of impending and immediate danger to all. I remember one particular situation while I was lifeguarding at an outdoor pool in Colorado. Afternoon thunderstorms, some very spectacular, were a common occurrence. We usually had plenty of warning when one was approaching, however, as distant lightning strikes could be seen as the storm approached from the west, billowing up over Pike's Peak. On one occasion, there was no such warning. Storm clouds were still a long ways off and there had been no visible flashes of lightning or sound of thunder.

That steady state of calmness changed both rapidly and dramatically as a large bolt of lightning struck a tree no more than three or four feet outside of the fence... and within fifteen feet of where I was standing! Believe me, my tuba-playing lungs spat out through that whistle for all they were worth, followed by, "OUTA' THE POOL!!!" (The latter not really being necessary; you've never seen fifty or so kids exit a swimming pool in such short order...)

The whistle then, in a general sense, represents our voice. It is our willingness to speak up for truth in a world which frequently prefers deafness and ignorance. We must be willing to stand up against the enemy's lies and twisted perversions of half-truths. As we do so, however, we must always remember to speak out of a right heart. Our hearts must be firmly grounded in both truth and mercy, always remembering that we once shared the same zip-code as those currently living in darkness. We must sometimes speak hard truth, but we must always speak it with a soft heart... a heart of mercy and grace. We must *speak the truth in love,* as Ephesians 4:15 puts it. The apostle Paul further exhorts us on this matter:

"Let your speech always be with grace, seasoned with salt, that you may know how you ought to answer each one."

Colossians 4:6

Now, salt here represents something which is pure... something which was used as both a preservative and as a healing poultice. In medical use, it served as both a topical antibiotic and to draw out infection and toxins from wounds. When used for this purpose, I am sure that it sometimes stung, but the aim was to bring about healing. And so it must be with our words, whether to non-believers or to fellow believers struggling with some particular sin. Speak the truth, but speak it in humility and love, with healing and restoration as the goal.

In speaking the truth in love, we must never place so much emphasis on what we perceive to be love that we forget the truth part. *I'm ok, you're ok* is a lie... Not one of us is yet perfected in Christ. All of us are in process and need both the DAILY grace of Christ and correction when we blow it. Salvation is a clean slate from past sin; it is not, however, a blank check to continue in sin! Jesus fully and completely forgave the woman caught in adultery, a capital offense in her culture. Although he had full right and authority to judge her guilty and condemn her, he did not. He did, however, *discern* her fallen state and upon pronouncing a full pardon for her past transgressions, exhort her to change course.

> "...Neither do I condemn you; go and sin no more."
> John 8:11

The Bible does indeed command us not to judge others, as many of those seeking to justify a sinful lifestyle will readily point out. This *judging*, however, speaks of declaring an ultimate, unalterable verdict or condemnation upon. It does *not* instruct us to walk through life blind and ignorant, pretending as some eastern religions do that sin and evil do not exist. God does in fact call us to be discerning individuals, alert and aware of sin's influence both in our lives and in the world around us... and we are called to confront it in both of these realms. Grace does not erase responsibility. More on this later.

"What then? Shall we continue in sin because we are not under law, but under grace? Certainly not! Do you not know that to whom you present yourselves slaves to obey, you are that one's slave to whom you obey, whether of sin to death, or of obedience to righteousness?"

Romans 6:15-16

The Rescue Line

Let us now move on to another piece of equipment employed in lifeguarding, the rescue line. The rescue line is simply a length of medium-weight rope twenty or so feet in length. One end usually has a loop which is held by the rescuer. The other end, which is thrown to the person in need of help, employs one or more buoyant floats, usually brightly colored and easy to see. The rescue line is generally used when the lifeguard sees someone who seems to be over-tired or beginning to struggle but is not yet in serious danger. It is thrown within easy reach and the person being assisted is to simply take hold and hang on while the lifeguard calmly tows them in.

The rescue line then represents general everyday words of encouragement and acts of kindness.

We should keep these close at hand, ever on the lookout for anyone in need of such assistance. Life beats us all down and a word of encouragement or act of what should be (but often isn't) ordinary kindness may be exactly what someone needs to keep their heads above water. That cashier who is taking a little too long, that waitress who makes a mistake on your order (or, the good Lord forbid, your bill!), that angry, rude, despicable co-worker... for all you know, their despicable behavior may simply be the spastic thrashings or exhausted malaise of someone sinking beneath the waves of a hopeless desperation.

That word of encouragement or act of kindness may just save a life. I have heard many stories of individuals contemplating suicide who changed their minds because someone simply took the time to speak a kind word to them. One of my classmates during my senior year of high school took his own life just a few weeks before graduation. He had always paraded himself as cocky, self-assured, and always "Mr. Cool". It turns out that, as is quite common, his true inner life was very different than the mask he wore at school. I cannot help but wonder if a kind word... a real effort to reach beneath that mask... may have made a difference.

This rescue line, employed correctly, may also be the tool God uses to draw others to salvation, but we must remember that there is a right way and a wrong way to employ this tool of the trade. Firstly, it is thrown *to* a swimmer, not *at* them. If you hit them in the face, you have failed. Our words of encouragement, acts of kindness, and other efforts of evangelism are to be offered to a lost world, not thrown *at* it. Always bear in mind that it is and must always be an act of their free will to reach out, take hold, and receive. God has never and will never force Himself upon anyone. How could we presume to be acting in His behalf if we were to do so? God is love and love, by its very nature, has to be received by an act of free will.

Once someone has taken hold of the rescue line, we must be wise in how we begin to draw them in. Many times it is best to allow them to simply rest and calm down where they are for a time with the assistance of the attached flotation devices. When we do begin to draw them in, our *tug* must never exceed their *grasp*. Don't jerk the rope out of their hands! The excitement of the opportunity to help a lost soul may tempt us to go off like a truth-bomb! If we do, however, we may very well lose that opportunity. Just as it was an exercise of their free will to initially take hold of the line, they must choose to continue to hold on. Learn the art of making them *want* to hear more... We are to be *fishers of men,* and any good fisherman knows how to work the lure to keep the fish interested but not scare them away.

Father God is extraordinarily patient, discerning, and wise in His dealings with us. He draws us in at a rate which we are personally able to handle. As His ambassadors to a lost and desperate world, we must exercise this same discernment and wisdom in our endeavors. We fish without hooks; the fish is free to let go at any time they choose to. We must always be ready and eager to share the grace, mercy, and TRUTH of Christ, but we must never attempt to force it upon someone unwilling or not ready to receive it. If we hit them in the face, we have failed. If we pull the lifeline from their grasp, we have failed. They will most likely end up worse off and more resistant to the Gospel than they were before.

Requiem of Silence

Alone I reside in a silent fortress, a solitary outpost of blackened stone. Fearfully secluded upon a mist-shrouded island adrift in the gray sea, I gaze out longingly through tinted windows. Locked alone in my tower of stone, I blend into the background of noise and din; just a shadow fleeting by, hugging the corners and the alleyways... alone in my silence, avoiding your gaze.

If only... if only one of you illumined ones would care enough to linger awhile. If you'd but stay your busy course long enough to notice my silent plea, hiding behind the walls of indifference and hostility. The arrows I sling protect my bleeding self.

That strange light you hide within, I know not its source, but I know my need. But you go flaming, flashing by... never noticing the desperate shadows. And so alone I sit in my tower of stone, bleeding still.

Lamentation

We had life...
life simple and complete,
filled with joy and peace
in their fullest measure.
No asphalt... but stone
and living waters
and flowered meadows.
No smog... but silver mists
and glassy seas
and unyielding tranquility.

But we chose a lie,
thinking God selfish.

And so all of our brittle days
we wander this maddening maze
grasping for Eden.

The Shepherd's Crook

There are times when a swimmer in trouble may require a firmer hand. When they are in a more advanced stage of panic or are actually beginning to submerge, the shepherd's crook should be employed. This is a long metal pole, eight to ten feet in length, with a wide, curved cradling *hook* on the end. It provides something more solid and substantial for the swimmer to grab onto. It may also be used by the lifeguard to `hook' the swimmer around the back so that they may be firmly and quickly towed in.

A few important safety precautions must be observed when utilizing the shepherd's crook. Most importantly, one must remember that it is *a long, hard metal pole.* As such, it is capable of injuring swimmers and others around you if you are careless in its use. It must be *aimed* accurately and with proper caution. If you frantically whack the swimmer you are trying to assist over the head with it, well... again... you have failed.

Secondly, the rescuer must be aware of their stance. They must shift their center of gravity, maintaining proper balance, and plant their feet securely on the deck. If you lose your balance and get pulled in, you have not helped.

Finally, the rescuer must maintain focus. There may still be several dozen screaming, splashing, rambunctious kids vying for your attention, but your ultimate responsibility at that moment is the one at the other end of that ten-foot pole. That is where your full attention must remain. If you allow your attention to be diverted, the one you are assisting may lose their grip on the pole, or you may lose your grip on them.

The shepherd's crook, then, represents the tool of *exhortation*. There are many verbs in the Bible which speak of letting someone know when they are doing things wrong – *warn, correct, rebuke, chastise*, and the like. All are, in some sense or another, degrees of this term "exhortation". The God we serve is all about redemption... about making things which have gone wrong right again. Any time He corrects, rebukes, or even punishes, it is always with the end goal in mind of restoring the one in error to a right path. May our heart hold this as its chief aim as well.

We spoke previously of the rescue line representing encouragement. Exhortation is a close cousin of encouragement, but it is specifically encouragement into a change of course or to a right action. It is a word of warning or correction spoken in love, hoping to turn another toward a right path. It is essentially saying, "I know you can get this right; let me help you." Depending on the occasion, it may lean more toward encouragement... or more toward warning... but the heart is the same in either case. Whether the lifeguard is using the rescue line or the shepherd's crook, his or her goal is to aid the swimmer, not drown them!

Far too many people in the church are afraid to confront. They have bought into the *just-be-nice* lie, forgetting all of those little episodes where Jesus knocked over tables and called people names. (See Luke 19: 45-46, Matthew 3:7, and pretty much all of Matthew 23 for starters.) This fear of confrontation comes from a wrong understanding and weak appreciation for what it means to actually love someone. Love is not a fluffy, warm, fuzzy feeling that makes you feel all giggly inside; it is a sometimes ruthless act of the will. It is choosing the highest long-term good for another even when that does not correlate with their highest level of comfort in the present moment.

God repeatedly allowed Israel to be conquered by foreign powers and sent into exile... even slavery... because He loved them! Read slowly through Psalm 78 sometime and see the incredible, broken-hearted love of God as he seeks to correct and redeem a wayward people who had fallen into every form of depravity and debauchery. See the furious love of a God who cared more for their long-term good than for their short-term comfort. It is not love to make someone comfortable with their sin. *Chocolate-covered cyanide is not a loving gift.*

I have a real problem with some of the things which are done in the name of compassion these days. Free "clean

needle" programs are one such example, where free hypodermic needles are distributed to drug addicts. This is ostensibly done to help keep them safe from being infected with certain diseases by sharing needles with others who may be infected. How about helping to free them from the disease and life-destroying slavery of drug addiction instead? We must be loving enough to confront the real problem. We must be willing to love others even if they hate us for it. Don't "love" them... *to death.* God holds us accountable in this.
(See Ezekiel 3: 17-21)

The degree to which we are able to speak correction to those around us will depend somewhat upon the depth and nature of our relationship to them. How much day to day contact do you have with this individual? Are they a co-worker, a family member, or someone you know from church? Are they a brother or sister in Christ, on the fence in this regard, or fully uninterested in the things of God? The strength of your connection to them in these ways will highly influence the effectiveness of this particular tool and the manner in which you implement it.

Let us now revisit those safety principles I mentioned a moment ago. I noted with some emphasis that the shepherd's crook must be used with proper caution and careful aim. This is most certainly true of exhortation. You must carefully consider your relationship to the individual in question. How likely are they to receive this kind of correction from you? Are there any potential relational obstacles such as workplace seniority which could become a difficulty? Do they have hot-button issues which you will need to tread carefully around?

Perhaps one of the most important considerations is this: What would be the proper time and place to bring up a given issue? Do not bring up a private issue in a public setting! Your aim should be to turn them away from a wrong path... to render aid, not to whack them over the head by shaming them in front of others. According to the specific issue there may be a need to involve others if they are not initially responsive, but always seek to keep the circle of correction as small as possible.

Do not fall into the trap of pursuing retribution if they have wronged you personally, but keep your heart set on restoring them to a right path. Only involve others if they do not respond to these efforts or the action in question is, in fact, a malicious criminal act. (See Matthew 18: 15-17)

I also noted that you must pay careful attention to your footing and to keeping your balance. These are crucial concepts in exhortation and correction. Ensure first of all that your footing is secure in both truth and grace. Are you really sure of the person's actions and heart in this particular matter? Many great offenses have been bred out of a simple misunderstanding. Perhaps you misheard something or are otherwise in error over their involvement in a certain matter. Perhaps they have received information or instruction of which you are not yet aware. Make sure that you have the facts and weigh whether or not this is something which requires intervention. Do not be hasty in acting and do not assume that you have all of the facts. Be willing to ask questions and to hear their side of the story.

Should confrontation be necessary, prepare through prayer and a humble heart. Are you seeing this fault in another because you have or have had a weakness in this area yourself? This is an extraordinarily common phenomenon. The most rabid anti-smokers are generally those who used to smoke themselves. Those who most readily recognize a speck in another's eye are those who have or have had a plank of the same species of wood in their own. Herein resides the opportunity to grow in both humility and empathy, both very godly qualities.

If you have experienced personal weakness in the same or similar area, you must be especially careful to be on guard and keep your balance. The enemy would love to use such an opportunity to drag you under again through the sin of pride. I am sure you have heard how that little indulgence generally precedes a fall...

We also need to be sure that we do not get pulled off balance should they resist or even openly reject the exhortation. Who likes to be corrected? Do not be surprised if they are offended. They may very well react with anger, resentment, and even retribution— verbal or otherwise. It is crucial that you do not react in kind. When we are called to confront, God holds us accountable to speak the correction. He does not hold us accountable to whether or not it is received. Do not be caught off guard by a negative reaction and pulled off balance into bitterness or resentment yourself. Be there to help and support them if they receive your words, but dust off your shoes and move on if not. (Matthew 10:14)

Be calm, firm, direct, and brief. Do not allow emotion to cause a bigger problem than what was there to begin with and do not feel that you must get them to agree with you at any cost. Speak the truth in love and allow their conscience to go to work from there.

A final consideration in speaking exhortation and correction is to keep a proper focus. This applies in at least two distinct ways. The first has already been hinted at... keep the goal in mind. Your aim should be to warn them away from a destructive path and towards the right way. It should be for their good.

Even if this *course correction* is uncomfortable or painful, you are living the love of Christ if you are faithful in this. A little discomfort now may just very well save them from much more later. *Godly sorrow* may very well be what is needed to guide them to a desired end.

> "Now I rejoice, not that you were made
> sorry, but that your sorrow led to
> repentance. For you were made sorry
> in a godly manner, that you might
> suffer loss from us in nothing. For
> godly sorrow produces repentance to
> salvation, not to be regretted; but the
> sorrow of the world produces death."
>
> 2 Corinthians 5:9-10

The second way you will need to maintain focus is in avoiding distractions and *rabbit trails...* side issues which in reality have nothing to do with the simple word of correction you are trying to speak. Often these come in the form of petty theological arguments or catch-phrases like the already mentioned, "You're not supposed to judge!" They may also manifest in such expressions as, "Well, I know I shouldn't, but..." and "I had to, because..."

The person facing an uncomfortable correction may even be clever enough to throw an innocent sounding inquiry into your path... something they are fairly certain that you will bite on... such as, "Well, doesn't the Bible say.....?" or "Well, the Hindus teach....." They may draw upon any number of humanistic or religious philosophies, all designed to subtly draw you off target until you don't remember what you came to talk about.

Having been a foster parent to several dozen troubled kids, I have seen many, many different shades and incarnations of this scheme, I assure you. Beware of these tactics and stay focused. Make it clear that if they have honest questions in these areas you are willing to address those questions *at another time*. Be careful not to get sucked into any pet-theological topics or arguments designed to get your hackles up. Once again, be calm, firm, direct, and brief.

> "Brethren, if anyone among you wanders from the truth, and someone turns him back, let him know that he who turns a sinner from the error of his ways will save a soul from death and cover a multitude of sins."
>
> James 5:19-20

Before leaving this section, it should be noted that should a fellow believer, or someone who claims to be one, refuses correction in a matter of obvious sin, the Word of God gives us clear and definitive guidance. Paul makes it clear in 1 Corinthians 5:9-13 that there is a clear and distinct difference between how we are to deal with sin among unbelievers we interact with and how we deal with it among members of the church. We should not be surprised by a person who is still in the dark about the things of God living in dark ways.

However, it is quite a different story for someone who should know better. It is tragic how many blatantly sinful lifestyles have become acceptable even among Christian circles, or those claiming to be. Let me be clear, if a believer is struggling with sin... as long as they are actually *struggling against it*... attempting to overcome it... your part is to encourage them, pray for them, and stand with them in solidarity. However, if they are simply choosing this sin, not making any effort to overcome it, that is a different story altogether.

Herein lies the difference between *willing* sin and *willful* sin. All sin is committed willingly, for we always have the opportunity to avoid it. (1 Corinthians 10:13) But even if we choose wrongly and commit sin, as long as we are willing to try again, grace is readily available. (1 John 2:1-2). However, it is possible for someone who is, or who claims to be a believer, to choose sin, fully aware that it is wrong, but not caring. You *can* be fully aware of truth... and yet reject it. One of the most terrifying passages of Scripture alludes to the awful fate which awaits someone who makes this most terrible of decisions... and holds firm to it until death.

If you have ever wondered what the unpardonable sin is, this is it... knowing the truth of grace and freely choosing to reject it. Since God will not force Himself upon anyone, even His mighty hands are tied in this case. If we come face to face with some unfortunate fool who has made this choice (sadly, I can say I have known one) we must simply walk away and pray that life's circumstances bring them home again before it is too late. We are not to have any further contact with them... To continue in any effort of friendship would both validate their choice to them and serve as a bad witness to unbelievers. Their only hope of rescue is in coming to their senses and repenting before it is too late. Any effort of yours to maintain an active relationship could only lessen the possibility of this.

"For if we sin willfully after we have received the knowledge of the truth, there no longer remains a sacrifice for sins, but a certain fearful expectation of judgement, and fiery indignation which will devour the adversaries. Anyone who has rejected Moses' law dies without mercy on the testimony of two or three witnesses. Of how much worse punishment, do you suppose, will he be thought worthy who has trampled the Son of God underfoot, counted the blood of the covenant by which he was sanctified a common thing, and insulted the Spirit of grace?"

Hebrews 10: 26-29

The Backboard

Finally, let us consider a piece of equipment which every lifeguard should be thoroughly familiar with, but hopefully never have to use... the backboard. The backboard is a buoyant support designed to safely secure, stabilize, and transport someone you believe may have suffered a spinal injury. It is usually about six feet long and wide enough to fully support an injured individual. Wide straps are used to secure the person being assisted and easy-carry handholds line both sides of the board. A cervical collar is frequently employed in conjunction with the backboard.

The lifeguard may have witnessed an individual being struck in the face, landed on by another swimmer entering the pool, surfacing unusually slowly after diving, or other such occurrence. Many times the victim will be conscious, but complain of back or neck pain or of tingling or numbness in their arms or legs. They may or may not show a visible sign of injury. Any person who is discovered unconscious in a pool should be considered a potential spinal injury victim, whether or not the lifeguard witnessed an injury event.

In whatever position or state the victim is discovered, special techniques are employed to properly align them for use of the backboard. Special care *must* be taken to prevent a possible injury from becoming worse! If a spinal injury *has* occurred, any rotation or pressure applied to the spine could result in paralysis or even death.

After the victim has been properly positioned, floating on their back in the water, a cervical collar may be applied. Then, the board is gently floated up underneath them. They are secured snugly to the board with a number of wide straps across their chest, waist, and legs. A strap is also secured across their forehead to keep their head from moving. They are then carefully transported to safety and attended while awaiting medical personnel.

Unless there is some kind of immediate danger, no potential victim of a spinal injury should be moved without first employing the backboard. The possibility of causing additional injury or even death is simply far too great. In desiring to aid the victim quickly, you must employ proper caution and patience. *Wisdom must be the master of compassion.*

This crucial principle most definitely applies to *ministering Christ in a messed-up world!* God is the most compassionate being ever to exist. His depth of emotion by far surpasses our ability even to comprehend. Yet this limitless compassion is in perfect subjection to a limitless wisdom. He has never and will never allow emotion to outstrip wisdom; to do so would be unloving and fully contrary to His nature.

As Christ's ambassadors, we must exercise that same wisdom. No one long inhabits this quite fallen world without suffering physical injury. The same is most definitely true of our emotional and spiritual selves as well. As we seek to share Christ with those around us, we will from time to time meet with extraordinary, unreasonable resistance. Even when someone initially shows interest, they may suddenly become resistant or even hostile.

It is far too easy to respond in kind to this hostility... but sometimes we need to look deeper. That festering hostility may just be a symptom of a deep and abiding wound. Perhaps we have unintentionally prodded too enthusiastically at a sore spot. Perhaps some Biblical truth we are presenting just does not... cannot... make sense to them because of some vicious, unhealed wound of which we are not aware. It may be quite difficult for someone to conceive of God as a loving, attentive father... if the only father they ever knew was a drunkard, abusive, or absent. For far too many in our modern world, "father" is not a nice word. A lifetime may be required to fully heal that particular wound.

It may be that an individual's negative reaction to "church" or "organized religion" is in response to a very real, very legitimate grievance. Many people are forever turned off to the pew experience due to having been on the receiving end of abuse... physical, sexual, or emotional... in that setting. Let's face it, there are a lot of phony religions out there, even phony so-called "Christian" churches. It may be a case of institutional theological error, or of a single pastor or other church leadership going `off the rails'.

A key tactic employed in warfare to destabilize an enemy nation is to give them lots of money... their money... in counterfeit form. To flood a nation's market with counterfeit currency will drastically decrease the value of the market and contribute to economic meltdown. The abundance of counterfeit currency destroys the value of the real thing in people's eyes. The real thing is no longer trusted due to the abundance of what is not real.

In the spiritual realm, this has been and will continue to be a key tactic of our enemy. He is a liar... a clever liar... but he has no creative power of his own. His key tactic is to counterfeit. The most seductive lies are those which look most like the truth from the outside. This may be an outright false religion, a theologically corrupt church, or a Christian leader... who truly *isn't* Christian.

If an individual has been the victim of a counterfeit church or of a counterfeit 'Christian', they are likely to be especially resistant to receiving the truth of Christ. Very few will slap their hand onto a hot burner a second time. Most counterfeit churches are very adept at employing the terminology of "Christianese", and you may find that terms such as *grace, Holy Spirit, fellowship, salvation,* or even *Jesus* invoke a profound misunderstanding or even negative reaction. In counterfeit churches, the meanings of these terms, which we readily understand, have been twisted and corrupted. We think that we are speaking the same language, but we read from different dictionaries. The time may come for you to explain in depth the correct understanding of these things in words, but you may find it more beneficial to simply live the love of Christ in front of them. When an intellectual understanding of Biblical truth is blocked by the scars of a counterfeit church experience, living Christ's love in front of them may still reach their spirit.

If an individual has, in fact, been a victim of some form of abuse in a church or religious setting, actions will *most definitely* speak louder (and more clearly) than words. You can say, "...But I'm not like that!!!" all you want, but they have most likely heard that before... and been lied to. Hearing that you are different will not help. They must *see* that you are different. Here is the ultimate test of patient perseverance. It is so much easier to say something than to live it, and requires a much more substantial investment of time.

An intellectual understanding of Biblical truth may be clearly communicated in words... in nouns, verbs, adjectives, and the like. Communicating a true *spiritual* understanding, however, is a much more difficult summit to conquer. It requires a much greater investment of time and of our very selves. It is also of much greater value. Here is the crucible of Christian ministry... a test of the genuineness of your love. This is what it truly means to *lay down your life for a friend.*

It may also be that an individual has been so beaten down by *life in general* that they are essentially emotionally paralyzed. Bitterness at what others have done to them... guilt over their own actions... a hopeless sense of defeat and failure over picking themselves up and falling again too many times... that laundry list of rejections and broken relationships...

All of these frequently lead to one desperately cold spiritual condition, summed up in the heart-rending question, "Why even bother?" We are told in Proverbs 13:12 that, "Hope deferred makes the heart sick..." and these poor souls are gravely ill, terrified to embrace hope even one more time. Too wounded to do otherwise, they *choose* bitter resignation and a frozen hopelessness. In their eyes, numbness is better than pain.

Any scar is clear evidence of a past injury. Whether a particular individual's scar manifests in anger, inappropriate levity, or resigned despair... we are dealing with a wounded person. In seeking to bring aid, we must exercise patience and wisdom in addition to compassion. If you sense that you are beginning to touch upon a wounded area, be very careful with how you proceed. Many times, by trying to help too much, you can cause greater injury; you can drive them farther away from God. Always pray and be patient and sensitive, seeking the right way and time to present truth which may prick a sensitive spot. You must also be very careful to maintain proper confidentiality. They should be able to trust you with sensitive issues.

A word of qualification here: NEVER agree to *absolute confidentiality!* Never promise, "I won't say anything, no matter what!" If there is a legal issue involved, or something which may be an immediate threat to their safety or the safety of others, it is your moral duty to speak out. In many states, it is actually a criminal offense to not report child abuse you have witnessed, or even have good cause to suspect. Absolute confidentiality in these kinds of cases would *not* be the loving or wise thing. You should make it clear that you will, to the best of your ability, help them work through a proper resolution to these issues, but will *not* help to cover them up. If there are issues which need to be brought out into the light, it is not a loving thing to keep them hidden in darkness, where they still have power over their souls.

However, in all other things, they should be able to trust you to *not blab their baggage!* Far too often, the prayer circle is a specious cover for gossip-gabbing! If you are a little too eager to 'share' something in this setting, perhaps you shouldn't. Perhaps you should check your motives. Many times, wisdom and godliness are expressed in silence. Don't lay another's dirty laundry out on the street for all to see.

As Christ's ambassadors, ministering to wounded souls, we should endeavor to follow His example of ministry. We should walk as He walked. Before His feet were ever once soiled with the dust of a fallen world, the hallmark of His life of compassionate ministry, guided by wisdom and patience, were foretold by the prophet Isaiah. As co-laborers together with Him, let us endeavor to follow in the Master's footsteps.

"Behold! My Servant whom I uphold, My Elect One in whom My soul delights! I have put My Spirit upon Him; He will bring forth justice to the Gentiles. He will not cry out, nor raise His voice, nor cause His voice to be heard in the street. A bruised reed He will not break, and smoking flax He will not quench; He will bring forth justice for truth."

Isaiah 42:1-3

Maintenance

Lifeguarding, of course, is not all about whistle-blowing and saving damsels (or dudes) in distress... Any lifeguard knows that maintenance is a big part of the job, although it is often unseen by the public. A lifeguard must have a keen awareness of their environment and how to maintain it in a safe and healthy state. Let us briefly examine this aspect of lifeguarding.

Testing the Waters

When you think of going swimming, water is certainly what first comes to mind. Most people, however, have no idea just how much effort goes in to testing and maintaining the water. A typical pool is tested at least daily for such aspects as temperature, PH, copper hardness, chlorination, and visual clarity. Chemicals such as muriatic acid, soda ash, chlorine, bromine, cupric sulfate, and flocculants such as sodium aluminate or calcium hydroxide are added in carefully calculated measures. Additionally, the water is constantly circulated through a complex heating and filtration system which, itself, must be maintained.

Although water *treatment* is not an issue for a beach-front lifeguard, testing still is. The beach-front lifeguard will routinely take water samples, testing for temperature and pathogens such as harmful strains of bacteria or algae. They must also be aware of potential hazards such as rip-tides, dangerous currents, submerged rocks, and such unwelcomed visitors as sharks and jellyfish. Although they have little if any direct control over these things, they are responsible to be aware of them and to inform and warn others.

This particular aspect of lifeguarding is a good reminder to test the waters in our own spiritual walk. The water in a pool or beach-front environment may **look** wonderfully inviting, yet be dangerously out of balance in some way. Similarly, spiritual influences in our lives may harbor dangers which are not immediately obvious. Just because someone speaks eloquently in 'churchy' words does not mean that their heart truly belongs to Jesus. They just *may* be a shark in sheep's clothing!

In my years of ministry I have seen many deceptive spiritual winds blow across the landscape. From time to time, certain books... or movies... or teachings have risen suddenly upon the scene and become 'the thing' to read... to watch... to follow, in order to be a part of the in-crowd of the church. Nearly all of these have sounded good and true on the surface, but somehow, in some way really difficult to put into words, were just somehow *'off'*. You see, even truth can be spoken in such a way as to make it lie. Truth spoken in a **wrong spirit** can be the deadliest of deceptions. We are warned about "winds of doctrine" in Ephesians 4:14.

A rather interesting account is recorded in Acts16:16-19. Paul and Timothy are preaching in the city of Philippi. On their way to prayer, a woman follows them, crying aloud, "These men are the servants of the Most High God, who proclaim to us the way of salvation." (vs. 17) You would think that they would welcome such attention, but Paul becomes highly annoyed... and shuts her up! Why? She was speaking truth... from a **wrong spirit!**

We are not told whether she was speaking in a mocking tone of voice; that is certainly a possibility. I have also heard it taught that a more grammatically correct translation would be that she said they proclaimed "A" way of salvation, and was somehow subtly insinuating that there were also other ways. In either case, she was definitely speaking from a wrong heart, and somehow serving the devil's purposes. Paul would have none of that and put a stop to it. We must walk in this same wisdom.

1 Thessalonians 5:21 is another passage which exhorts us to carefully analyze those voices which would speak into our spiritual lives. We are encouraged to examine those things which may appear as truth, but in reality be clever lies. We need to weigh these voices, especially and most importantly against the truth of God's Word. We should, "Test all things; hold fast to what it good."

In Acts 17:10-12, Paul actually commends the Jews in Berea for not taking his words at face value, but searching the Scriptures to verify what he was saying. If any prophecy, counsel, teaching, or spiritual philosophy contradicts the Word of God in any way, that prophecy, counsel, teaching, or spiritual philosophy is to be discarded--- whether that contradiction can be quantified in words, or simply seems to be spoken out of a wrong spirit. We are of course responsible to warn others in a loving way if we sense that something is unscriptural or seems spoken in a wrong spirit. If we sense that there might be sharks in the water, we need to speak up.

"Beloved, do not believe every spirit, but test the spirits, whether they are of God; because many false prophets have gone out into the world."

1John 4:1

Cleaning the Filter

In every pool, a filtration system is employed to help keep the water clean and clear. And yet, the filter itself eventually becomes too full of impurities to function properly. In performing its job of cleansing the pool, the filter itself will regularly need to be cleansed. Fresh water is pumped through the filter in the opposite direction and impurities are flushed from the system.

Similarly, the filter of our minds cannot help but accumulate crud from the world around us. Despite our best efforts to focus on what is good and pure, (see Philippians 4:8) open sewers of mental and spiritual filth litter the landscape around us. Impure thoughts and attitudes are hopefully filtered out before they become our words and actions... but a residue usually remains. That built-up residue must be regularly flushed from the system by confession, repentance, and a good, wholesome application of fresh "water of the Word." (see Ephesians 5:26)

This is a daily necessity, pictured in the Bible through the custom of foot washing. You see, one simply cannot walk around dusty middle-eastern streets all day in open-toed sandals... with horses, camels, and donkeys everywhere... and keep clean feet. Despite your best intentions and desires, soiling will happen. Fortunately, our Savior still washes the feet of His disciples.

Clearing the Deck

The liquid environment is not a lifeguard's only responsibility. They are also tasked with *clearing the deck.* This refers to keeping a safe environment outside the pool or on the beach. Shoes, towels, and trash must be picked up and dealt with. If no one drowns on your watch... well, that *is* a fine thing. But, if someone gashes their foot on a broken bottle or trips on a hose and breaks their arm, you have performed your job less than admirably.

In our own personal and ministry lives, we must also be conscious to keep the decks clear. We must be aware of any actual or potential stumbling blocks and do whatever we can to clear them away. This pertains both to us personally and to others we are in relationship with.

For us personally, this would speak to having an awareness of those things which are likely to trip us up. We are all still in the process of spiritual *growth*. This means that we have not yet arrived at perfection! We still have areas of weakness and things which may tempt us. I guarantee you that the enemy of our souls is intimately familiar with these areas of weakness. We must be as well...and be on our guard against them. This world is a mine field; we must follow the map God has provided and stay alert.

Clearing the deck also clearly speaks to our relationships with others. If you have wronged someone, you obviously need to make it right. If someone has wronged you, you should do your best to extend grace, believe the best, and move on. However, there are times when something will just elude your ability to get past... when something will just *stick in your craw.* If an offense becomes a stumbling block and a barrier to an open, godly relationship, you will need to go to that person and deal with it. It may have simply been a misunderstanding or a bad day... Whatever the issue, pray first and deal with it quickly before what may be a minor issue becomes a festering wound and a root of bitterness. Take some time to consider Matthew 5:23-24 and Matthew 18:15-17. I have personally seen these gems of the Word implemented and work miracles in restoring broken relationships. I have also seen them *ignored*, resulting in catastrophic injury and even a church split.

Finally, the topic of *clearing the deck* speaks quite clearly to being cautious to not lay stumbling blocks for others. As I have already stated, we are all in a place of growth, and thus still all less than complete in understanding and maturity. Something which you personally may have no issue with may be a major stumbling block for another. Movies, music, alcohol, or even a simple deck of cards... all can be, unfortunately, topics of hot contention in Christian circles. I have even known people who refused to play "Yahtzee" because it used dice... and dice were used in 'that other game'... so dice were evil! No, I am not making this up.

My exhortation to you is this: Do not allow your freedom in Christ to put others into bondage. Whether or not something is wrong by the letter of the law, it is wrong *by the law of love* if it causes another to stumble. If your conscience tells you that there is nothing wrong with having a beer with dinner... fine... just don't down that frosty one in front of someone recovering from alcoholism! Don't imbibe that brew in front of a baby Christian (or hardline, ultra-conservative Pentecostal) who believes that even *root* beer is of the devil... You must value relationships above rights. If what you consider your right causes another to stumble in their faith, your *right* is *wrong.*

(See 1Corinthians 10:23-33)

Always a Hook

There's always a hook
when the dark one offers
something to entice;
what feeds the hunger
fostered by flesh
carries a pitiful price.

There's always a lie
to lure you back
to that which you forsook;
before you bite
you should consider...
there's always a hook,
always a hook,
always a hook.

Two Men

Two men, living in one skin,
battling for control...
One must die, the other shall fly
to the champion of their soul.
To realms of light,
in star-blazed flight
to dance before the throne;
precious gems we are to Him,
who kneel to Him alone.

But first the flame, first the fight...
first the pain, and first the night.

First the race, and then the prize.
First the dust, and then the skies.

Until that day, we yet remain
battling the darkness,
overcoming the pain;
two men,
living in one skin,
battling for control.

Clay

I am nothing,
empty, a void, waiting to be filled---
time, space,
and potential...
a blank page, waiting eagerly
upon the grand designer
to render some useful scheme;
to breathe new light and music
into the dark silence.
I had fancied myself the potter---
I am but clay.

As with Adam, dear and sovereign Lord,
lay your hand upon me... shape me to
your good pleasure and impart to me
that eternal essence--- that spark which
with time grows into a glorious dawn of
purposeful joy. Grant me the fierce
grace to lie silent and still as your all-
knowing skill prods and pokes and
tears and transforms... until I at last
take on the true expression of your
faultless design.

Training and Conditioning

We have to this point taken a brief look at the tools of lifeguarding and how they may serve as metaphors for certain principles of ministry. I assure you that I could expound at greater length, but I hope that this brief treatment may prove to be of some value. Let us now move on to examine, in like manner and spirit, some of the various aspects of training and conditioning involved in this same profession.

Study

A great deal of training is required to be an affective lifeguard. Obviously, one should know how to swim! You cannot always count on someone being within easy reach of the shepherd's crook or rescue line. There will be times when you need to enter the water.

I can honestly say that I had never taken a swimming lesson until I began my first Advanced Life Saving classes. I was a fairly decent swimmer already, but had learned the rudiments in a rather unorthodox manner at the age of five. We lived in Cascade Locks, Oregon at the time, where the Columbia River spans a good bit more than a mile between the shores of Oregon and Washington.

While wading in the shallows of the marina one hot summer afternoon, I stepped off a rock and suddenly found myself in much deeper water. A strong current suddenly began sweeping me out toward the middle of the river, as a barge cruised upstream in my direction. It was very much a matter of, "Swim or die..." I did manage to survive... obviously... but purely through the application of what I would refer to as *the panic-stroke.*

Once I began training as a lifeguard, I would learn and practice somewhat more advanced techniques, such as the breast-stroke, the side-stroke, and the forward crawl. These allow one to move through the water in a much more efficient manner than the *dog paddle*...or the *panic-stroke*. Knowing what you are doing is a good thing.

While I firmly believe that relying on the direct leading of the Holy Spirit is an essential aspect of ministry, I also realize that training and study are necessary components. If you are going to lead a squadron of soldiers into battle, a field radio is a good thing to have; you can speak directly to headquarters and receive necessary information and direction. However, that radio is not the sole required piece of equipment. Unless you are an invincible one-man army like *Wolverine,* you are going to need a gun. You are going to need bullets. You will need to have a good map to follow and proper training.

We must be trained and equipped for ministry as well. Every believer should have a thorough and growing knowledge of Scripture. Yes, we are promised the leading of the Holy Spirit, and the Holy Spirit can reveal to us specific information or insight which we have no other way of knowing. However, one of the Spirit's primary functions is to *remind us* of Biblical truth we have studied and to give us wisdom as to how it applies to a current situation. To put it simply, the Holy Spirit cannot remind you of something that you've never bothered to study. If you've never put it *in,* He cannot bring it *out.* (See 2Timothy 2:14-19. 2Timothy 3:14-17, and John 1:25-26)

Serving

Training and study should also involve a heart of servanthood exercised in behind the scenes roles. You may see this as on the job training. No true disciple of Christ needs a spotlight. We should all be willing to serve in whatever way will build up the Kingdom...not our own egos. We should all be willing to learn ministry by serving others who are in leadership. By holding up the hands of others, we not only play a crucial role in ministry, but learn the true heart of a disciple and servant of Christ. (See Exodus 17:9-13) To God, there is no one person more important than another. Leadership is simply a different role, not a better one. It is responsibility, not privilege. The pastor of a church has different roles and responsibilities than the custodian, but let that custodian shirk their duties and things will not function well for long. Both are necessary. Both have value. A true servant of Christ serves wherever they can contribute...in the spotlight, or the broom closet makes no difference.

Many heads of major corporations started out in the lowliest of jobs. Through beginning their careers at the bottom rung of the ladder and working their way up over time, they have built a true awareness and understanding of the jobs they now supervise others in performing. You cannot truly be a good leader if you are not first a good follower. This applies to ministry the same as it applies to business. Be willing to serve those above you...and those below you... and you will learn ministry in the best way possible.

Specialized Training

In some fields of ministry, specialized training may be a necessity. If you are going to serve overseas, language and cultural training will probably be required. Believe it or not, smiling and making eye contact is considered to be a threatening gesture in some cultures! In other cultures, if you shake hands incorrectly or allow your feet to point directly at someone, you could be in real trouble. I remember practicing the correct head-shakes in a mirror in Bulgaria. In this eastern European country, up-and-down means "NO" (Neh...) and left-and-right means "YES" (Da'). Yes, that took some getting used to! Da'!

The first place of ministry my wife and I served together following our marriage was in a camping program for the handicapped and developmentally disabled. This involved a *great deal* of specialized training. There was a great deal of very specialized first-aid training, as well as behavioral management and observational techniques to learn. We had to learn how people with a wide variety of mental and physical restrictions communicated their needs and desires and how to affectively respond.

We also had to learn and practice how to tolerate and deal with certain things that in normal, everyday life would drive you batty! Some campers possessed certain compulsions over which they had little, if any, control. We needed to be able to recognize and tolerate these, such as excessive touching of our faces or the absolute need to follow a precisely ordered routine without the slightest variation. Some inappropriate actions such as pinching or hitting could be redirected. Others, we simply had to endure, such as one camper who literally laid awake all night saying the word, "WEDGE"...

In any field of ministry, you must always be willing to learn. Those who think that they know it all are usually the ones who know the least. Keep a humble heart and be eager to learn from those already serving in a given field of ministry of culture. If specialized training is necessary, by all means, do not neglect this training.

Staying Safe

One very important aspect of training for a lifeguard is learning *releases* and *escapes*. When entering the water to assist a swimmer in distress, you must exercise extreme caution. A panicking person will grab desperately at anything that floats. That includes you! In order to maintain safety and control should you be grabbed, you must learn certain techniques.

A *release* is when you break a swimmer's grip on you, but maintain physical contact, most commonly with a wrist hold. You can then help to calm them and position for a wrist‑tow, cross‑chest carry, or other assistance. Several forms of releases must be learned and well‑rehearsed so that they can be implemented quickly. They must become almost an automatic reflex.

When a swimmer is at a higher level of panic or is much stronger than you, you may need to use an *escape* maneuver. This is when you not only break a swimmer's grip on you, but sever any direct physical contact. You *escape* out of their reach. You can then attempt to verbally calm them and do whatever necessary to safely assist them. The crucially important distinction here is that you may grab hold of them, but they are not to grab hold of you.

The most extreme form of an escape move is known as *plunging*. This is when you intentionally plunge underwater with someone who has a firm grip on you which you cannot break. As I stated earlier, a panicking person will grasp at anything which *floats*. If you are no longer floating, they will almost certainly let go of you and try to scramble for the surface. We refer to this instinctive impulse as "climbing the ladder". Once they have released you, you are then free to regain your own composure and attempt once again to assist them.

The crucial ministry principle here is maintaining proper control of a situation. When you are ministering to or counseling with desperate people, they may have a tendency to drag you under with them. They see that you float and are likely to grab at you desperately. This may mean that they attempt to place undue burdens on you, expecting you to fix all of their problems. They may have racked up enormous debts, monetary or emotional, over a period of years...but in their desperation, expect you to fix it all in a day. They may have been severely irresponsible in their personal lives and expect you to rebuild all of the bridges they have burned. They don't really want *help,* they want a magic genie.

In these cases, the only way you can really help them is to get them to start acting responsibly. They need to repent of wrong and look to God as their source, not you! If they have racked up debts, they need to make them right. If they have burned bridges which they shouldn't have, they need, with God's help, to work on rebuilding those bridges themselves. Many times, they know what the right thing is, but don't want to do it. They want someone else to do the hard things for them. But, my friend, this is not how you grow. If you want to *be* right, you must not only *know* right, you must *do* right. You see good...you do good...you become good. This is the message of Philippians 2:12-16 and James 1:22-25.

Information + Application = Revelation

In order to properly assist someone in distress, you must maintain control. Give no place to undue burdens of guilt or a martyr complex. God is God, you are not. If you really want to help desperate people, you will remember this and seek His guidance and wisdom as to how much you should... or shouldn't... intervene in a situation. Sometimes they need to face a plunge, to be willing to place their hope not in you, but in God. As I stated earlier in this book, wisdom must be the master of compassion. If they drag you under with them, you are not truly helping.

Endurance

Endurance conditioning is an important part of lifeguarding. Physical strength is a positive attribute, but operates somewhat differently in the water than on dry land. Endurance, the ability to simply continue, is of greater importance. If you've ever seen the Disney – Pixar movie, "Finding Nemo", then I am about to get a song stuck in your head. Are you ready.....?

"Just keep swimming...
Just keep swimming..."

Sorry about that! But it does make a good point, and one relative to this discussion. Many times in lifeguarding... in life... in ministry... what makes the difference between success and failure, between life and death, is the simple determination to keep on keeping on. There will be long, hard work days. There will be less than comfortable living conditions. There will be poor internet service. There will be frustrations, persecutions, discouragements, and genuine failures. You may face weeks, months, or even years in ministry with no apparent progress or fruit to encourage you in your labors. Those you are trying to help may continue to foolishly jump back into shark-infested waters every time they make it safely to shore.

So what's a person to do? Just keep swimming... Get used to the idea that there will be times of great difficulty in this life, because we are not home yet. We may glimpse the distant shore, but it is a long way off yet. Keep your head above water and simply endure. Jesus Himself gives us this exhortation:

"These things I have spoken to you, that in Me you may have peace. In the world you will have tribulation; but be of good cheer, I have overcome the world."

John 16:33

For more on this, see Hebrews 10:32-39, James 1:2-4, 2Timothy 2:1-13, Isaiah 40:31, Psalm 103, and 2Corinthians 4:7-16... just for starters!

The Brick

Probably the severest test of endurance in lifeguard training is the dreaded brick. There are required daily minimums for lap swimming, timed tests, and underwater search and recovery drills, but perhaps the most difficult test is... *the brick!* You are required to swim out into the deep end of the pool holding a ten-pound, rubber-coated weight. When the instructor blows their whistle, you are required to tread water for extended periods of time, holding the brick above your head with both hands. You have only the use of your legs to keep you afloat and if your lips touch the water once, you fail.

This was a requirement of the final exam when I received my Oregon State lifeguarding license and you only got one attempt at it. To pass this test requires the utmost focus, determination, conditioning, and a stubborn endurance. And so it is with life, and with ministry. Those who finish the course are those who keep their eyes on the prize and simply refuse to give up. They are the blessedly stubborn, who are determined to endure... to persist, no matter what storms may come. An ancient mariner's song says it well:

The briny deep may boil and roll,
but it shan't lay claim my soul.

A Dozen Do-Nots...

At the conclusion of this book, I would like to share briefly about the specific ministry with which my family and I currently serve. Just prior to that, however, I would like to attempt to wrap up this little study by presenting a few general principles of life and ministry. I will attempt to be as brief as possible, as I have already more freely expounded than I had intended to when beginning this project.

Each of these topics could very well be developed into a full-length book of their own. I will endeavor not to do so... at this time! I will simply present each principle as briefly as possible and offer a few Scripture references helpful for further study and meditation. Innumerable references could be considered applicable for each topic, but I shall list only a few, trusting that God will personally lead you to others as you meditate on those particular starting points. Thank you for investing your time in this study. I pray that the principles presented herein enrich you personally and help to foster a more fruitful life of ministry to our blessed Savior and soon-coming King.

Michael M. Middleton,
YWAM Faith Harvest Helpers

A Dozen Do-Nots

1. *Do not swim with sharks.* The Bible has so very much to say about choosing our friends wisely. A good part of our strength and safety as Christians comes from our friendships with fellow believers. Yes, each of us *will* have numerous associations with unbelievers. Indeed, we could hardly claim to be extending the love of Christ to an unsaved world otherwise. The important principle here is that we are to guard our hearts. We are to choose

our *close associations* wisely and make sure that we are positively influencing those around us who are unsaved. We are to be influencing them for the Kingdom, not allowing them to influence us for the world. Do not allow the darkness of the world to dim the light of Christ within you. Any relationship which would do so must be set aside.

(Proverbs 12:26, Proverbs 13:20, Romans 12:21, 1Corinthians 5:9-13, 1Corinthians 15:33, 2Corinthians 6:11-18, 1Timothy 6:3-5)

2. *Do not play with jellyfish.* Christ came to pay a costly ransom in His own blood that we might be forgiven. His forgiveness sets us free *from* sin; it does not give us liberty to continue *in* sin. Freedom from sin is both a one-time event *and* a daily struggle. Make sure that you are fighting on the right side of that struggle. If you play with fire, you will get burned. If you play with jellyfish, you will eventually get stung.

(Numbers 32:23, John 10:10, John 12:46, Romans 6:1-14, James 1:13-16)

3. *Do not swim in the mud.* Guilt is a killer. Condemnation is a paralyzing venom. Once you have repented of sin, you must lay its guilt on the altar of grace and leave it there. Cradle it no more in your bosom, but release it to the fires of God's limitless compassion. To indulge its anguish any longer would simply hinder your freedom in Christ and maintain a stronghold of darkness in your heart. You have been cleansed, don't swim in the mud; it is the devil's snare.

(Psalm 51, Psalm 103:1-6, Romans 8:1-4, John 1:9, ICorinthians6:9-11)

4. *Do not swim alone.* When we were saved, we became part of a family. That family is essential to finding and fulfilling God's call on our life. The fellowship, encouragement, and accountability of godly relationships keeps us safe, gives us strength, and brings joy to the heart of God. Sheep live in flocks; it is the sheep who wanders off alone who falls prey to the wolf. Jesus is the good shepherd, and intends his sheep to stick together.

(Proverbs 17:17, Proverbs 18:24, Proverbs 27:6, Proverbs 27:17, Hebrews 10:24-25)

5. *Do not get tangled in nets.* Funding is an inevitable part of any ministry endeavor. As we pursue the responsibilities of meeting the requirements of this particular aspect, we must beware of ungodly entanglements. Whether funding comes from churches, individuals, government or corporate grants, we must be on the guard against 'strings' which would entangle. If any funding source would lay upon you requirements contrary to God's call or standards---pass---and trust God to provide through other means.

The devil will use any net he can to entangle and hinder your ministry. If he can use money with strings attached, he is more than happy to do so. When applying for grants, especially through government agencies, I have always insisted on one strategy: "It's ok for this money to be frosting, but we must never allow it to be the cake." Discernment and discretion are crucial necessities to avoid the shipwreck of getting tangled in nets.

(Proverbs 2, Psalm 112:5-7, Ephesians 5:15-17)

6. *Do not swim on an empty stomach.* At first, this may sound like blasphemy to anyone with a background in

lifeguarding. After all, we've always been told not to go swimming right after we've eaten, right? Well, I am of course speaking in a spiritual sense here. I speak in terms of ministry. You cannot give out what you yourself have not received. Keep your spiritual tanks filled up so that you can, out of the overflow, minister Christ to others. Spend regular daily time in God's presence through studying His word, through meditating upon the wonders of His creation, and through the increasingly difficult to master discipline of stillness.

There is nothing sacred about the word *busy.* Skyrockets burn brightly and put on quite a show in their brief, frantic lives... but leave behind nothing but smoke and ashes. They bear no lasting fruit. Instead of burning out and leaving only ash, learn to nurture the seed of Christ within you through study, prayer, and quietness. Fruit will then flow naturally through your life and ministry.

(Psalm 119:11-15, Psalm 4:4, Psalm 46:10,
 Psalm 91:1-2, Matthew 8:23-27, Luke 5:15-16,
John 10:27, Romans 1:20, Philippians 4:6-8)

7. *Do not get stiff.* Flexibility is perhaps one of the most crucial keys to a life in ministry. If you are not going to collapse into a quivering pool of misery, bitterness, and self-pity, you must learn to embrace a life of flexibility. Finances, your daily schedule, living conditions, authority structures... your ability to cope with ever-changing circumstances *will* be tested. If you are going to stay sane and have any hope of a fruitful ministry, you must learn to be organized, yet flexible.

(Acts 10, 1Corinthians 9, Philippians 4:11-13)

8. *Do not neglect your equipment.*

I have already spoken at some length about the *tools of the trade* in lifeguarding and how they relate to ministry. In addition to practical and intellectual equipping for ministry, certain spiritual equipping is a must. If you hope to have an affective ministry, these tools must not be neglected. Learn them. Use them.

(Ephesians 6:10-24)

9. *Do not forget the fun.* Too many perceive a sanctified life as one of a lemon-sucking sourpuss. Yes, a life in ministry is often difficult, demanding, and sometimes disappointing, but it is also a joyous life. If you allow the weight of ministry to freeze your face into a perpetual sternness, you are not reflecting the nature or character of Christ. God has a sense of humor. Our God is a God of peace and joy. Joy can sometimes be a difficult

choice, but it is a righteous one.

(Nehemiah 8:9-12, Habakkuk 3:17-19, Psalm 30:11-12, Psalm 89:15-18, Psalm 95:1-7, IPeter1:6-9)

10. *Do not get a big head.* We sometimes will find ourselves ministering to some really messed-up people. Do not ever forget that you have been at some point just as messed-up... perhaps in different ways, but messed-up all the same. Not one of us deserves to escape the flames of hell, let alone walk the streets of glory. You have been *forgiven*; it's all grace. Never forget that. The only "special" in you is Christ. If it becomes difficult for you to remember once having been in a quite fallen state, then it is quite likely that you may find yourself in that fallen state again.

(Psalm 39:4-5, Isaiah 40, Romans 7,
 ICorinthians 15:9-10, Galatians 2:20-21)

11. *Do not become an idol.* One of the most sinister temptations in ministry is to allow yourself to become an idol. An idol is something which takes the place of Christ in another's eyes. Our role as ministers of Christ is to point people to Christ. If we, in meeting the very real needs of a fallen world, allow someone to see us – not Christ - as their *source,* we have failed. We are only a channel of God's grace and goodness, not its source. We can sometimes be tempted to do *too much* for people or to receive *too much* gratitude for help given. In either case, we risk becoming an idol, and God has ways of dealing with idols. He may have to allow us to topple. We must point people to Christ. We must teach them to rely on Christ and to look to Him as their source, not to us or the ministry we represent. We are only the friend of the Bridegroom.

(John 1:19-27, John 3:22-30, Acts 14:8-20)

12. *Do not forget 'forever'.* Every one of us has been born into a fallen world. The weight of this world and the discouragements we face herein can, most certainly, be difficult to endure. And yet, those of us who can truly call ourselves Christians have experienced another kind of birth. We have been born from above.

A child's eyes are not fully developed at birth. Months pass before the optical muscles grow strong and really learn how to focus. Then, the child finally begins to see clearly. In like manner, those of us who have been born into the Kingdom must learn to see clearly... to see things in the light of eternity. The great pioneer missionary and Christian martyr Jim Elliot recorded in his own private journals, "He is no fool who gives what he cannot keep to gain that which he cannot lose."

Like this great man of God and countless others like him, we need to learn to properly focus, to see beyond what is now... and here... Whatever being a follower of Christ may cost us, whatever our sacrifices in life and ministry, it is nothing in the light of forever. The tiny seeds which we are privileged to plant in this life will one day bear a precious harvest in eternity.

(Psalm 27, Psalm 37, Psalm 92, Psalm 93, Psalm 97, Revelation 20-22)

The Gift Giver

He planted a tree in the barren wilderness and nourished it with life-giving showers. Deep within the secret places of the earth He formed the iron, and gave men the knowledge and skill to refine and forge it, and to cast it into the heavy mallet and fierce, flesh-rending spikes. The thorny bush which was hastily crafted into a regal mockery grew in some forgotten corner of a courtyard by His command and sovereign care. The star which heralded His birth and the darkened, bloody moon which grieved His death... before the breath of life ever entered Adam's lungs, the sovereign Lord set them in their places in the heavens with clockwork precision. And when He climbed that barren and bloody hill on that fateful day, His life was surely not taken from Him; He gave it away.

New Every Morning

Ancient twisted oaks stand somber as creamy orange light spills across the frosted meadow, sparkling like the night sky. Stripped of distractions, I sit silent and still, embracing the rude essentials. *The sparrow... the lilies of the field;* I begin to understand God at the root--- in His elemental presence--- independent of mortal perception. Love, mercy, serenity... all of these He simply is, radiating life and blessing regardless of whether we open ourselves to receive it. Joy and simplicity---these are His eternal essence. Like the warmth of sunrise after a cold night, it is sure and certain... and could not be otherwise.

Grace Alone

Beauty, chaos, creation, decay, order, destruction, rage, serenity, fear, hope, despair and renewal... all tied up together like some great cosmic knot--- this is the world as we have made it, a fabled treasure hidden somewhere within the briar. Every joy fades and every pleasure has a price; everything we build perseveres for but a fleeting season before time and circumstance scatters it to the wind.

What bitter fruit was spawned in Eden when first we chose to disbelieve. Its dark seed has grown throughout the ages to confuse and choke the simplicity which was always the Sovereign's plan. We sweat and toil and bleed, trying to meet some nameless need, and know too late we never can... for the garden was grace--- and grace alone redeems. It was not for toil, but for love He fashioned man.

Echoes of Tomorrow

There's a new world coming. Beyond the flames of ignorance and greed, beyond the cries of despair and the schemes of hateful men, do you hear it? Can you hear the trumpet's voice and the song of Moses and of the Lamb? Do you hear the joyful shouts of the redeemed... echoes of tomorrow?

Can you hear the approaching hoof-beats, pulsing faster... faster... faster... like the heartbeat of a lovesick God, half mad with passion for His bride?

Can you sense; do you know the fire in His eyes... the fires of passion and rage, ready in an instant to pour out vengeance upon the destroyer of men's souls?

There's a new world coming, and the heavens will soon pass away at the voice of His command.

Faith Harvest Helpers

A Ministry of Youth with a Mission

Sharing Food ~ Giving Hope

Introducing Faith Harvest Helpers:

"To know God and to make Him known..." This is the motto and the guiding principle of Youth With A Mission International. Within this framework, Faith Harvest Helpers plays a vital role in *sharing food* and *giving hope*. Processing and distributing food as well as medical supplies and other essentials to needy people at home and worldwide, Faith Harvest Helpers is a vital and growing ministry centered around the principles and aspirations of Matthew 25:35... "For I was hungry and you gave me something to eat, I was thirsty and you gave me something to drink." It is this heart of servant-evangelism in meeting the needs of a hungry world –both physical and spiritual- which defines YWAM Faith Harvest Helpers.

Beginnings...

For over 20 years, members of Faith Harvest Helpers have made the yearly trek to YWAM Gleanings in California to help glean and process food which is sent to hungry people around the globe. During one of these trips, a vision was born to do something with surplus food in the Pacific Northwest. In 2006, Faith Harvest Helpers incorporated as a 501c3 and began processing surplus salmon from Washington State waters to share with those in need. In 2010, we grew to include a distribution center located in Yelm, Washington where fresh fruit, vegetables, bread, and dairy products could be distributed as well.

Growing...

Locally, approximately one million pounds of donated food is now processed and distributed by members and volunteers of Faith Harvest Helpers annually. This includes vegetables, bread, fruit, salmon, and dairy products. This is distributed by a small army of volunteers to benefit Pacific Northwest food banks and feeding programs.

Globally, we partner with a variety of other ministries to distribute non-perishable food, Christian literature, medical supplies, hygiene items, and other commodities with a message of hope.

Looking towards the future, we plan to acquire a farm property in the vicinity of Yelm to convert into a new and expanded ministry center. This will allow us to consolidate all ministry operations into one location, thus maximizing efficiency and good stewardship of resources. It will also vastly expand the opportunities for ministry and growth.

Construction plans include warehouses, dorms, kitchens, a chapel, administrative offices, a training and discipleship facility, and large greenhouses. As plans unfold, we will be growing much of our own food to supplement donated items, utilizing state- of-the-art hydroponic technology.

We will also develop a commercial cannery for fish and other commodities and continue in the role of "making disciples" through YWAM's Discipleship Training School.

Jump on board!

For information on how to volunteer, donate, or join an outreach, please contact paul@faithharvesthelpers.org.

You are also invited to visit our website: www.ywamfhhwa.org.   Additional contact information is provided at the website.

Made in the USA
Middletown, DE
03 July 2023

34500460R00070